THE STRUGGLE OF THE MAGICIANS

G. I. GURDJIEFF

Scenario of the Ballet

THE STRUGGLE OF THE MAGICIANS

Act One

THE ACTION takes place in a large commercial town of the East.

The market square where various streets and alleys meet; around it, shops and stalls with every variety of merchandise—silks, earthenware, spices; open-fronted workshops of tailors and shoemakers.

To the right, a row of fruit stalls; flat-roofed houses of two and three stories with many balconies, some hung with carpets and others strewn with washing.

To the left, on a roof, a tea shop; further on, children are playing; two monkeys are climbing on the cornices.

Behind the houses are seen winding streets leading to the mountain; houses, mosques, minarets, gardens, palaces, Christian churches, Hindu temples and pagodas.

In the distance, on the mountain is seen the tower of an old fortress.

Amongst the crowd moving about the alleys and the market square, types of almost every Asiatic people are to be met with, clad in their national costumes: a Persian with dyed beard; an Afghan all in white, with proud and bold expression; a Baluchistani in a white turban with a sharp peak to it and short white sleeveless coat with a broad belt, out of which stick several knives; a half-naked Hindu Tamil, the front of his head shaved and a white and red fork, the sign of Vishnu, painted on his forehead; a native of Khiva wearing a huge black fur cap and a thickly wadded coat; a yellow-robed Buddhist monk, his head shaved and a prayer-wheel in his hand; an Armenian in a black 'chooka' with a silver belt and a black Russian forage cap; a Tibetan in a costume resembling the Chinese, bordered with valuable furs; also Bokharis, Arabs, Caucasians and Turkomans.

The merchants cry their wares, inviting customers; beggars with whining voices beg for alms; a sherbet vendor amuses the crowd with a witty song.

A street barber, shaving the head of a venerable old 'hadji,' recounts the news and the gossip of the town to a tailor who dines in the adjoining eating house. A funeral procession passes through one of the alleys; in front is a 'mullah' and behind him the corpse is borne on a bier covered with a pall, followed by the women mourners. In another alley a fight is in progress and all the boys run there to watch. On the right a fakir with outstretched arms, his eyes fixed on one point sits on an antelope skin. A rich and important merchant passes along ignoring the crowd, his servants follow him, carrying baskets laden with purchases. Then appear some exhausted beggars, half-naked and covered with dust, evidently just arrived from some famine area. At one shop, Kashmir and other shawls and materials are brought out and shown to customers.

Opposite the tea shop, a snake-charmer seats himself and is at once surrounded by a curious crowd. Donkeys pass by, laden with baskets. Women walk along, some wearing the 'chuddar' and others with unveiled faces. A humpbacked old woman stops near the fakir and with a devout air, puts money into the coconut almsbowl standing near him. She touches the skin on which he is seated and goes away, pressing her hands to her forehead and eyes. A wedding procession moves by; in front are gaily dressed children, behind them buffoons, musicians and drumbeaters. The towncrier passes, shouting at the top of his voice. From an alley is heard the din of the copper-smith's hammers. Everywhere there is noise, sound, movement, laughter, scolding, prayers, bargaining—life bubbling over.

Two men separate themselves from the crowd. Both are richly dressed. One of them, Gafar, is a handsome, well-built, wealthy Parsi about thirty or thirty-five years of age, clean shaven except for a small black moustache, and close-cut hair. He wears a light yellow silk coat belted with a pale rose-coloured scarf, and blue trousers; over this a brocade robe, the skirt, cuffs and facings of which are embroidered in silver; on his feet are high boots of yellow leather, the legs embroidered in gold and precious stones; his head is covered with a turban of a figured Indian material, its predominating colour is turquoise blue; on his fingers are rings with large emeralds and diamonds. The other man is his confidant Rossoula, dressed equally richly, but carelessly. He is short, stout, subtle and cunning, the chief assistant of his master in all his love affairs and intrigues. He is always in a sly and merry mood. On his head he wears a red skull-cap with a yellow turban wrapped round it; in his hand is a short red rosary.

Gafar looks at some of the wares and stops occasionally to speak with some of his acquaintances, but evidently nothing interests him. In all his movements one can see the pride of a man satiated with pleasures. To his equals he is patronizingly civil, but on everyone else he looks with contempt or aversion. He has experienced everything, seen everything, and the things for which other people struggle and exert themselves no longer exist for him.

At this moment, two women come out of a side street on the left into the square. One of them, Zeinab, is young, about twenty or twenty-two years of age, of an

Indo-Persian type, more than average height and very beautiful. She is dressed in a white tunic with a green scarf round her waist; her smoothly-dressed hair parted in the middle is bound with a gold fillet; thrown over her head she wears a 'chuddar,' but her face is uncovered. The other is her confidant, Haila. She is a short, plump, middle-aged, good-natured woman. She is dressed in a blue velvet coat under a violet 'chuddar.' Her mouth is covered with a handkerchief.

Zeinab holds a roll of parchment wrapped in a silk handkerchief. She passes along the square, graciously giving alms to the beggars whom she meets. Gafar notices her and follows her with his eyes. Her face interests him because it seems, at the first glance, to remind him of someone or something. He enquires of Rossoula and other acquaintances who she is, but no one knows.

Just then, Zeinab goes up to a beggar woman near whom stands a half-clad boy about eight years old with an open sore on his naked arm. As she gives him alms, Zeinab notices the sore, and bending over him she speaks sympathetically to the beggar woman about him. Finally she says something to her, pointing to one of the side streets and then to the boy. It is evident from her gestures that she is advising the woman to take the boy where he can be cured.

All this time, Gafar does not cease to observe Zeinab.

Zeinab wishes to bind up the boy's arm, but she has nothing to wrap round it, so she unfolds the silk handkerchief in which the rolls of parchment are wrapped and binds it round the sore. Then, accompanied by Haila, she leaves the square by a side street.

Gafar quickly consults Rossoula. It is evident that he is giving him instructions to follow Zeinab and to find out what he can about her. When Zeinab has disappeared, Rossoula follows by the same street. Gafar stands looking after him, then slowly goes up to the beggar woman and begins to talk to her. Recognizing the handkerchief on the boy's arm as the gift of Zeinab, he, without knowing why, desires to buy it. He offers the woman some money, but she refuses to sell it. Gafar, thereupon, throws down a handful of money and takes the handkerchief almost by force from the boy, then slowly walks towards the middle of the square. The astonished woman excitedly picks up the money and raising her hands to heaven, thanks Gafar. Then, taking the boy by the hand, she goes down the alley pointed out by Zeinab.

Rossoula returns and with deprecating gestures, tells Gafar that he has discovered that Zeinab is not a woman whom it is possible to approach casually. Then, still talking together, Gafar and Rossoula go out by one of the streets on the left.

Above: The tea shop on the roof. Below: Zeinab binds the boy's arm.

Evening draws on. In one of the alleys there is much movement, and out from it comes a dervish accompanied by a crowd amongst whom are many women and children. This dervish has been much honoured in the country of late, and he enjoys great respect amongst all the different nationalities. He recites some sacred verses and to the rhythm of the verses he makes certain movements resembling gymnastics or a dance.

The meaning of the verses is:

God is one for all,
But he is three-fold.
Men err, because he is seven-fold.
In his totality he is one-sounding,
In his division he is many-sounding.
And in another division he is contradictory.
He is everywhere in all forms.
When men see him
It depends on their qualities
Which part they touch.
But who touches, if he is ignorant,
Sees in the part he touches, all of him,
And not doubting, preaches about him.
He sins already
Because he acts against
The laws laid down

In the commandments of the Most High.
The commandment is this:
I am truth.
Your unbelief draws you
Into nearness with me
Because he who sees me. . . .

The end of the verses is lost in the loud beating of drums round a charlatan selling medicines.

The twilight deepens. One by one the merchants collect their wares and close their shops. At the moment when the movement of the crowd is at its height the curtain falls.

Act Two

In the school of the White Magician.

A spacious room which looks like a laboratory or an observatory with here and there shelves on which stand boltheads, glasses and objects of fantastic shape recalling modern apparatus, also several parchment rolls and books.

At the back, an enormous curtained window. To the left, a door leading to an inner room. To the right a door leading outwards.

In the right-hand corner stands an hour-glass. At the left-hand side stand low tables on which there are more boltheads, glasses and open books.

In front of the window stands a telescope of strange form, and to the left, on a small table, is an apparatus similar to a microscope.

To the right stands a large throne-like chair, with a high back on which is portrayed the symbol of the enneagram, and at the left side is a small chair for the Magician's assistant.

When the curtain rises there are several pupils, both men and women, already on the stage and others are seen to enter from time to time. They are well-built, nice-looking young people with good and pleasing expressions on their faces. They are dressed in white tunics; those of the girls are long, those of the men, to the knee. On their feet are sandals. The girls have their hair dressed smoothly and bound with gold fillets, the men wear silver ones. All have scarves round their waists; those of the girls are yellow, orange and red, those of the men are green, dark blue and light blue.

They are all occupied. Some are arranging and cleaning the apparatus, some are reading and others are shaking certain liquids in glasses. By now, the number of pupils has increased.

Through the outer door the Magician's assistant enters. He is an old man of medium height, wearing spectacles and with a short thin grey beard. He wears a robe of yellow over a short white under-garment with a violet-coloured scarf round his waist. On his feet are sandals; on his head a white skullcap with a violet-coloured scarf wound round it. In his hands he holds a long rosary of mother-of-pearl, and on his breast, hanging from a silver chain, is the symbol of the heptagram—a seven-pointed star in a circle.

The pupils greet the Magician's assistant who responds

graciously while going from one to another examining and correcting the work. The pupils continue to assemble. It is evident that the relationship between them all is kindly, gracious and friendly.

A servant enters through the inner door and says something, and from the movements of those present it is obvious that they await someone.

The White Magician enters. He is a tall well-built old man with a benign and pleasant face and a long white beard. He is dressed in a long white robe with broad sleeves and facings beneath which is seen a cream under-garment. On his feet are sandals. In his hand is a long staff with an ivory knob, and on his breast hanging from a thick gold chain, is the symbol of the enneagram worked in precious stones.

To the deep bows of the pupils the Magician replies with a kind smile as he blesses them. Then walking slowly to the throne, and after again blessing the pupils, the Magician sits down. (At this moment the symbol on the throne lights up.) The pupils each in turn, come forward and kiss his hand, after which they return to their places and resume their interrupted occupations.

At this moment Zeinab enters. She is late and out of breath from hurrying. She goes up to the Magician and also kisses his hand. By the way in which the Magician greets her, it is evident that she is one of his favourite pupils. She then goes to the other pupils and apparently imparts to them her recent impressions of the beggar woman with the boy.

One of the pupils goes up to the Magician, who is talking with his assistant, and asks him to explain something. Evidently the Magician's answer interests everyone, for gradually they all collect round him and listen. Continuing the explanation the Magician rises (at this moment the symbol on the throne is extinguished) and going to the microscope he starts some demonstrations. The pupils in turn go up to the microscope and look through it. Afterwards, the Magician goes to the window and draws back the curtain. The clear starry sky is seen. The Magician directs the telescope towards the sky. The pupils in their turn go to the telescope and look through it, at the same time listening to the explanation of the Magician.

The chief idea of the exposition is as follows: What is above is similar to what is below, and what is below is similar to what is above. Every unity is a cosmos. The laws which govern the Megalocosmos also govern the Macrocosmos, the Deuterocosmos, the Mesocosmos, the Tritocosmos and others, inclusively down to the Microcosmos. Having studied one cosmos, you will know all the others. The nearest cosmos of all for our study is the Tritocosmos, and for each one of us the nearest subject of study is oneself. Knowing oneself completely one will know all, even God, since men are created in his likeness.

Having said this, the Magician slowly returns to his throne.

The servant enters, and approaching the Magician, informs him that someone is asking leave to enter. Having received permission, the servant brings the beggar woman with the child. She throws herself at the feet of the Magician and begs for help, pointing to the boy. Zeinab also goes up to the Magician and intercedes for the boy.

The Magician, after looking at the wound, speaks to two of the pupils who then go into the inner room and return, one carrying a cushion on which lies an ivory wand with a large silver ball at one end, and the other carrying a handkerchief, a cup and a jar containing some liquid. The Magician takes the jar and pours the liquid into the cup, steeps the handkerchief in this and lays it on the wound. Then with great care he takes the wand and, without touching the wound, passes the wand several times over the boy's arm. When the Magician takes the handkerchief off, the sore is no longer there.

The beggar woman, struck dumb with astonishment, falls on her knees and kisses the edge of the Magician's robe. The Magician strokes the boy's head caressingly, and then dismisses them.

The pupils disperse to their places and resume their occupations. The Magician walks about the room, going to some of the pupils to examine their work and give suitable instruction. After some little time, he says something to all of the pupils and returns to his throne.

Immediately the pupils leave their work and place themselves in rows, and at a sign from the Magician they go through various movements resembling dances. The Magician's assistant walks up and down and corrects their postures and movements.

These 'sacred dances' are considered to be one of the principal subjects of study in all esoteric schools of the East, both in ancient times and at the present day. The movements of which these dances consist have a double purpose; they express and contain a certain knowledge and, at the same time, they serve as a method of attaining a harmonious state of being. Combinations of these movements express different sensations, produce varying degrees of concentration of thought, create necessary efforts in different functions and show the possible limits of individual force.

During an interval, one of the pupils points to the hour-glass, whereupon the Magician tells them all to finish their previous occupations and prepare themselves for what is to follow. Meanwhile he himself goes to the window and raises the curtain.

It is early morning and the sun is rising on the horizon. As the first rays appear, the White Magician with his assistant and his pupils behind him fall on their knees. They pray.

The curtain falls slowly.

Act Three

In the house of Gafar.

A room with an alcove in the right-hand corner, in which—behind carved columns—can be seen a fountain with a marble basin.

To the left, a door leading to the inner apartments, and at the back, another door leading to the garden.

The room is arranged in the Perso-Indian style. At the right, benches covered with rugs and cushions are placed in several tiers against the wall Mindari. In the left-hand corner is a low divan near which are several fretwork tables. On one stands a kalian and other smoking appliances, on another a sherbet set, on a third a small gong and on a fourth a jug and basin of exquisite and costly workmanship for washing the hands.

Gafar is walking about the room. He is without a robe but on his head is a skullcap adorned with precious stones. His every movement, his every glance show that he is waiting impatiently. Occasionally he sits on the divan and becomes absorbed in thought. He feels that quite new things are happening to him. He who has always been so haughtily calm and indifferent is now agitated and worried by trifles which before would not even have attracted his attention. Of late he has become irritable, suspicious and impatient.

Just now he is waiting for Rossoula who is to bring him news concerning Zeinab, the woman whom they met in the bazaar a month ago and whom Rossoula—in spite of all his skill and experience in such matters—has not yet succeeded in enticing into Gafar's harem. Yesterday Gafar ordered Rossoula to arrange this at any cost and what disturbs him so much now is the expectation of the result of Rossoula's final efforts. But at the same time, he feels that all this is simply ridiculous. Many times before he has been attracted by some woman, but while Rossoula has been busying himself in the matter, either he forgot about the woman or she ceased to interest him. But now, not only does he not forget but every day he thinks more and more about Zeinab.

Rossoula enters by the door at the back. He seems very distracted—and this is quite unnatural for him. He brings very discouraging news. He tells Gafar that all his efforts to fulfil his orders have failed and even he does not know what more to attempt.

They both reflect deeply. Every means of enticing Zeinab has been tried; everything has been done that can be done in such a case. They have sent her the most varied gifts: ancient Indian fabrics embroidered in gold; the finest horses—Arab, Chinese and Persian; Siberian furs; such a rarity as a priceless emerald necklace—the gift of the Rajah of Kolhapur to Gafar's grandfather; Gafar's famous blue pearl, the 'Tear of Ceylon'; and lastly, they have offered her for her very own—as a separate harem with menservants and maidservants—the renowned castle of the Gafars, the pride of their family, the 'Breath of Paradise.' But all has been in vain. Zeinab has refused everything and will listen to nothing.

Gafar is perplexed. He becomes more and more convinced that he has not the strength to reconcile himself to Zeinab's incomprehensible stubbornness and he understands that, in truth, she has been the cause of his unusual mental state during this time. It is evident that in this woman there is something exceptional. The way in which he, Gafar, receives all Rossoula's failures amazes himself. In any other case he would simply have been indignant, but now although he is unable to suppress his anger, in his heart he is almost glad that in this case all Rossoula's ordinary methods are insufficient.

The strange things which he observes in himself turn his attention to his relationship with women in general.

Thanks to his riches, his eminence and the circumstances of his birth, his life has been so arranged that, even at seventeen, he was already surrounded by women and—in accordance with the custom of his country—he had his own harem. At present he is thirty-two but still unmarried, in spite of the fact that for a long time he has wished to marry, especially to please his old mother who is always dreaming of his marriage. But until now he has never met any woman who, according to his views, is suited to be his wife. Many women have attracted him and in the beginning have seemed devoted and deserving of his trust, but in the end all have shown that their love and devotion have only been masks beneath which have lain petty egotistical feelings. With some it had been the passion for a young and handsome man, with others the thirst for the luxury which he could procure for them, with others again, the vanity of being the favourite of a nobleman and so on.

All that he has seen has utterly disenchanted him. He has never known a woman for whom he could feel the trust and esteem which, according to his views, should belong to his wife. He has become accustomed to look on all the fine words about love and the sympathy of souls as the mere fantasy of poets and gradually women have become more or less alike for him, differing only in their types of beauty and in their varying manifestations of passion. His harem has become part of his collection of precious things. He could no more live without his women than he could live without smoking, without music, or without all the luxury which has always surrounded him. But he has long ceased to look for anything more in woman than the momentary enjoyment of a beautiful thing.

And now, suddenly there has arisen within him this strange curiosity towards this incomprehensible woman. Can it be possible that she is in truth so utterly different from all others? Zeinab's appearance had impressed him at the first glance, but what more does he know of her? According to the information obtained by Rossoula, Zeinab is the only daughter of a rich khan of a distant town. She is twenty-one years old and completely free, not betrothed to anyone, and she lives alone very quietly, with some servants and an old woman called Haila. At home she occupied herself with sciences and she came here in order to study at the school of a celebrated magician. This school she visits every day and the remainder of the time she spends at her house engaged in her studies. In all this there is much that is strange, unlike anything to which he has ever been accustomed. But the thought of Zeinab gives him no rest; he cannot stop thinking of her and he is prepared for any sacrifice to gain possession of her.

Still thinking deeply, Gafar gets up and walks about the room. Then, evidently in the grip of a new thought, he seats himself once more on the divan.

It is now clear that it is impossible to seduce Zeinab by means which attract other women and conquer their resistance. This being so, there remains but one thing to do—to marry her. Sooner or later he must take a wife, and a more beautiful one than Zeinab he will never find. And if she should prove to be such a wife as he has dreamed of then it will be happiness for him and joy for his mother.

Gafar thinks thus for some time and finally speaks of his decision to Rossoula. Then he summons a servant and gives him an order. The servant goes out by the door on the left.

Soon after an elderly woman enters by the same door. She is one of Gafar's nearest relatives. He explains his decision to her and begs her to undertake the part of matchmaker. The old lady says she will carry out his commission with pleasure and has no doubt of success. It is well known that all the most famous beauties of the country would count it a happiness to become his wife, knowing of his wealth and position. She goes back to the inner apartments and presently returns accompanied by two other women. All three, veiled in 'chuddars,' then set out for Zeinab's house.

Gafar, with a thoughtful expression, still sits on the divan. Rossoula walks about the room and from time to time turns to Gafar suggesting various distractions. But Gafar's thoughts are far away and nothing attracts him. He listens to Rossoula in an absent-minded way and finally, only to get rid of him, agrees to one of his suggestions.

Immediately on Rossoula's orders, musicians enter forming an orchestra of assorted Afghan, Indian and Turkestan musical instruments. These instruments are: a zitera (a kind of balalaika with a long finger-board with seven strings, played on with a bow), an adoutar (a kind of balalaika with two strings, played with the fingers), a rabab (with three gut strings and three copper strings, played on with a small wooden pick), an atarr (a kind of mandolin with a long finger-board and seven strings, played as a mandolin), an asaz (also a kind of mandolin with three silk and three gut strings, played as a mando-lin), a caloup (a kind of zitera with many strings of steel and copper, played on with a bone pick worn on the thumb), a zourna (a kind of pipe), a gydjabe (a kind of violin), a daff (tambourine), a davul (a kind of drum), a gaval (a kind of flute), a galuk (a kind of clarionet), and others. The musicians seat themselves on the Mindari and begin to play.

As soon as the music starts, the dancers of the harem make their appearance entering by pairs, dancing.

These dancers have all been brought from different

countries. For their beauty, as well as their skill and agility, they are considered to be the finest in the land. People have come from afar simply to see them. No stranger seeing their group dances could help being enraptured by them, and when each one dances the dance of her own country, the cleverest judges are moved to ecstasy.

There are twelve dancers, all of them dressed in their national costumes. Today, either because they feel the mood of their master or because it is long since they have danced before him, they dance with exceptional abandon.

First, a Tibetan performs one of the dances of her mysterious fatherland. Next, an Armenian from Mousha dances to the accompaniment of slow music an amorous dance of her country, almost drowsy, but full of hidden fire. She is followed by an Osetinka of the Caucasus in a dance light as air. Then a Gipsy, a daughter of the people who have forgotten their homeland, in a burning, whirling dance seems to speak of the freedom of the steppes and the distant fires of the camp. After her, an Arabian, beginning slowly then quickening and quickening her movements, attains a mad pace, then suddenly relaxes and gradually swoons in ecstasy. Then a Baluchistani, a Georgian, a Persian, an Indian nautch girl—each one by her movements—manifests the soul, the nature, the temperament and the character of her country.

Musicians and dancers try to entertain Gafar

Gafar, indifferent to everything else, has always delighted in his dancers, but today he looks at them almost without seeing them so completely is he immersed in his thoughts and feelings.

During one of the group dances the women envoys return. With a contrite look the old lady tells Gafar that his proposal is not accepted. Gafar becomes mad with rage, chases everyone out of the room and remains alone with Rossoula. They are both silent.

Gafar strides up and down the room. He could have expected anything, but not this. It is beyond everything. Never in his life has he had to experience such a humiliation. Rossoula is no less thunderstruck than Gafar. He stands in deep thought, and is evidently racking his brain. Presently his face clears and he goes up to Gafar and speaks to him.

Gafar listens with a gloomy face. What Rossoula proposes goes against his deepest feelings, but he is insulted and indignant and wishes at all costs to have his own way. His desire for Zeinab has almost turned to hatred, and the wish to have revenge for his humiliation over-powers him. Rossoula continues to persuade him. Finally, after a short struggle with himself, Gafar consents.

They call a servant and send him with a message.

Gafar again seats himself on the divan with a morose

and wrathful expression. Rossoula wanders about the room rejoicing in his inventiveness and resource.

After a short time, an old sorceress enters accompanied by the servant.

She is short and bent with a large hooked nose, tousled grey hair and lively roving eyes, swarthy-faced with a large hairy wart on the left cheek; her long, thin, sinewy hands have long dirty nails. She is dressed in a short soiled coat of violet colour and black trousers; on her feet are old Turkish slippers; she is covered with a dirty black 'chuddar' patched in many places with coloured scraps; in her hand is a plain stick.

Gafar asks the sorceress whether she can bewitch a woman into falling in love with him. The sorceress, with self-confident expression, replies affirmatively, but when she hears the name of the woman, she trembles with fear and says that in this case she is powerless. They offer her gold, but this time gold does not help.

The sorceress is unable to do anything herself, but she tells them that there is one person who, if he wishes, can bewitch Zeinab. It may be possible to persuade him, but it will be necessary to give him much, much gold.

Gafar and Rossoula consult together; they question the sorceress and evidently decide to set forth at once. The sorceress consents to guide them.

The servant enters and helps them on with their outer

garments. Meanwhile, by Gafar's order, servants bring from the inner apartments bags filled with gifts. Then, accompanied by the servants carrying the bags, Gafar and Rossoula go out by the door at the back. Curtain.

Act Four

The school of the Black Magician.

A large cave. The back wall has a projection in the middle; to the right is an ascent to the entrance, to the left, a passage leading to an inner cave.

At the left-hand side in a dark recess is a kind of hearth or stove in which a fire is blazing. On the stove is a cauldron out of which clouds of greenish smoke escape occasionally. In front of the stove sits a shaggy half-naked creature who stirs the fire with a three-pronged fork of strange shape and now and then throws wood into the stove. In a niche above the stove is a human skeleton and more curiously shaped forks project from one side. In the centre of the cave, towards the back, stands a large stone shaped like a throne-couch. On a pole above it is a symbol of the pentagram.

Hanging from the ceiling are various stuffed animals— an owl, a toad, bats, also human and animal skulls.

Here and there stand low tables with various objects scattered on them, and boltheads, glasses, books and rolls of parchment are lying in disorder about the cave.

A boa-constrictor glides around at liberty and black cats walk to and fro.

This is the school of the celebrated Black Magician.

When the curtain rises some of his pupils are moving about the cave; others are sitting down. A few are laying out cards as though telling fortunes; some are studying the lines of each other's hands, and some—collected in a corner—are preparing potions.

The pupils are men and women of varying ages, some young, others older, but all of unpleasing appearance. One or two are deformed, thin with disagreeable shifty eyes, dishevelled hair and warts. The movements of all are sharp, angular and jerky. Their attitude towards each other is hostile and derisive. They are dressed in a slovenly fashion in short violet-coloured coats and black trousers. On their feet are Turkish slippers. The only difference between the dress of the men and the women is that the women wear belts of black cord and have black handkerchiefs on their heads. Some of them are tattooed on the face and hands.

One of the pupils near the throne begins slowly to make strange, rhythmic movements which apparently please the others, for one by one they leave their various occupations and join him. As their number increases the movements quicken and become more and more varied and gradually they form themselves into a ring and begin to revolve madly round the throne. At the moment of greatest frenzy a noise and a knocking are heard at the left of the cave.

Instantly the ring breaks up. Disordered movements and bustle follow. Jostling one another with fear, the pupils rush back to their places and snatch up their former occupations trying to give the impression that they have never interrupted them.

From the inner cave the Black Magician enters. He is a man of medium height, lean, with a short half-grey beard, black eyes with long eyelashes and thick unkempt hair. His movements are jerky with a characteristic manner of his own, his glance is contemptuously piercing. He is dressed in a short black silk coat beneath which is seen a glowing crimson under-garment a little longer than the coat. On his feet are Turkish slippers; on his head a black skullcap. In his hand is a long whip, and on his breast, hanging from a black silk cord, is a golden pentacle.

At the Magician's entrance all fall on their faces. He goes to the throne without looking at anyone; on the way he even steps on one of the pupils. He seats himself. (The symbol above the throne lights up at this moment.) He throws open his coat, baring his breast and his belly. The pupils in turn go up and kiss him on the belly. With a kick he knocks one of them over. The others with

35

cowardly malevolence mock at the fallen one.

When the ceremony of kissing the belly is ended, the pupils at the Magician's order, place themselves in rows to right and left of him and at a sign from him they begin to perform various movements.

During one of the intervals the old sorceress comes in through the outer entrance with a candle in her hand. She goes slowly and fearfully up to the Black Magician, kisses him on the belly and says something to him in a cringing manner, pointing towards the entrance.

After a moment of reflection the Magician nods his head in consent. The old woman goes out backwards and quickly returns with Gafar, Rossoula and the two servants carrying the sacks of gifts. The servants come in trembling with fear and looking about them with astonishment and horror. When they reach the centre of the cave they throw down the sacks and rush head-long away. Rossoula and even Gafar feel almost as much fear as the servants.

Gafar goes up to the Magician and tells him what he wishes. The Magician listens but when Gafar mentions the name of Zeinab, he absolutely refuses to do anything whatever, knowing, like the sorceress, that Zeinab is a pupil of the White Magician.

Gafar persists. Pointing to the sacks he pulls out his purse, draws a ring from his finger, takes off precious jewels and throws all before the Magician.

At the sight of the gold and jewels the Magician hesitates, and finally consents to cast the spell if Gafar can obtain something that has recently been in contact with Zeinab's person. Gafar reflects, then suddenly remembers the silk handkerchief which he bought from the beggar woman, and drawing it out he gives it to the Magician. The Magician points to the corner of the cave and bids him wait. Then in a powerful voice he gives some orders to his pupils.

Some of them move a table into the centre of the cave and cover it with a black cloth bordered with the signs of the Zodiac and Kabalistic symbols, worked in red. Others go into the inner cave and bring out various objects including an ebony wand with a gold ball at the top and a lump of soft clay which they place on the table. Next to the clay they place, opened, a thick book with strange hieroglyphics and the symbol of the hexagram and an urn, out of which projects a human thigh bone.

The Magician takes off his garment, receives some unguent from one of the pupils, smears it over his body, resumes his garment and over his usual dress puts on a robe with very wide sleeves. The robe is bordered all round with the signs of the Zodiac; on the back is embroidered the symbol of the pentagram, on the

37

breast a skull and crossbones. On his head he places a high pointed head-dress embroidered with large and small stars.

Then he takes Zeinab's silk handkerchief and crumpling it up places it in the middle of the lump of clay, from which he models the likeness of a human figure. This he places on the table. Next, on the floor around the table, he draws a large circle within which all the pupils collect. The Magician stands near the table and gives a certain order to the pupils. They immediately form themselves into a chain, men and women alternating. The man standing on the Magician's right and the woman on his left, take hold of his elbows with their free hands. Some of the pupils remain outside the chain.

The Magician takes the wand in his right hand and with his left he makes certain movements and whispers incantations.

It is seen that the pupils in the chain contort themselves, making convulsive movements; some of them become weak and even fall. Their place is speedily taken by other pupils outside the chain who try to do this as quickly as possible so that the chain may not be broken.

The clay figure on the table gradually begins to light up, at first faintly, then more strongly and more brightly.

Two pupils are working at the stove; one constantly throws wood into it, the other stirs it up. The fire in the stove grows fiercer, long tongues of flame shoot out from it.

As time goes on, the movements of the pupils in the chain become ever more violent and terrible; they are evidently exerting their utmost strength. The Magician himself is making an intense effort.

The clay figure lights up ever more and more strongly when the wand passes near it, and at intervals it gives out bright flashes. Above the cauldron a noise is heard which gradually increases, and at the moment when the noise becomes very loud, the light in the cave becomes dim and suddenly—above the stove—the shadow of Zeinab appears and slowly lights up. As the shadow brightens the steam escaping from the cauldron decreases. The flame in the stove burns even more fiercely. The sphere on the wand and the clay figure give out strong intermittent flashes. The Magician and all the pupils in the chain are terribly convulsed. The noise in the cave increases and becomes like claps of thunder and, at one of the terrible explosions, the cave is plunged in darkness.

Little by little the light re-appears. The shadow of Zeinab above the cauldron can no longer be seen. The flame in the stove has died down. The pupils, utterly exhausted, lie on the ground. Even the Magician is half-lying on his throne, weak and spent. One by one the pupils begin to rise. The less exhausted among them give the weaker ones something to drink and help them to rise.

The Magician having partially recovered, takes the clay figure, wraps it in a rag and gives it to Gafar with some instructions.

All that has happened has produced such an overwhelming impression on Gafar and Rossoula that at first they cannot move. However, after a while, with dragging footsteps they go out accompanied by the old sorceress.

The Magician, by now fully recovered, takes the sacks with the gifts and scatters them on the ground. The pupils with wild rejoicings fling themselves on them and snatch them up, after which they dance in a ring round the Magician.

In the midst of the wildest dancing the curtain falls.

Act Five

The same scene as the Second Act.

When the curtain rises the White Magician and all his pupils with the exception of Zeinab are present.

The Magician and his assistant with whom he is talking are watching the pupils who, placed in groups, are performing movements resembling dancing.

Suddenly Haila rushes in, falls on her knees before the Magician and with excited gestures hurriedly tells him what has happened to Zeinab.

What she relates is so unexpected that at first the Magician can scarcely understand what she is trying to tell him. He is amazed. Reflecting deeply he rises and walks about the room. The pupils, too, are astounded. From time to time the Magician turns to the old woman in order to ask more details of the situation.

Finally he comes to a decision, and turning to his pupils he makes a proposal to them. Several of them express agreement. The Magician, having chosen one of them, places him on a chair, takes both his hands and looks into his eyes. It is seen that the pupil gradually falls asleep. When his eyes are closed the Magician makes several passes over him from head to foot. The pupil is now in a hypnotic sleep. The Magician puts several questions to the sleeping man. By the movements of his lips it is seen that the pupil answers. The room becomes half-dark.

The purport of the sleeper's answers is reproduced in a series of pictures which appear on the back wall.

Zeinab's room. She is alone. Each of her postures and movements, every expression of her face, bears witness to some powerful struggle within her. Sometimes she springs up and walks nervously about the room; at one moment she appears to conquer what torments her, at the next, overcome by something stronger than her reason, she falls helpless on the divan. She is suffering terribly; this is evident from her gestures which are full of grief and despair. At times it seems as though she were defending herself against something; her mind is stubbornly resisting a strange feeling or desire which has entered into her.

Haila, on entering, does not recognize her mistress, so entirely has Zeinab changed towards her. She hardly notices Haila, and to the old woman's words and entreaties she either pays no attention at all, or else replies with impatient gestures. The old woman goes out with a crestfallen expression.

Zeinab's torture has no end; the struggle within her increases and increases. Mixed feelings of fear, desire, curiosity, shame, alternate more and more rapidly within her. Now becoming very excited, then suddenly growing weaker, she hurries from spot to spot and can find no resting place for herself.

At the moment of her greatest agitation Rossoula enters, bearing a tray of jewels from Gafar. Zeinab is not in the least astonished at this unusual visit, on the contrary, it seems as though she had expected it.

Rossoula, after presenting the gifts, speaks to Zeinab, who with nervous agitation, questions him. She takes the jewels, and in an excited and automatic manner tries them on before the mirror. Rossoula, meanwhile, is trying to persuade her to some course to which she finally consents.

Haila again enters. She is amazed and can understand nothing, so unusual is all this for her. Realizing at last what is happening, she throws herself on her knees before Zeinab, imploring her not to consent to Rossoula's entreaties. But Zeinab appears completely changed. Impatiently tapping with her foot, she orders the old woman to be silent. Then rapidly throwing a cloak round her, she goes out with Rossoula.

Haila remains distracted, not knowing what to do.

Suddenly she comes to a decision, puts on her shawl, and goes out hurriedly.

The picture vanishes. The ordinary light returns.

The Magician moves away from the sleeper and walks about the room, greatly perplexed. His assistant, making several passes over the sleeper from foot to head, awakens him, and one of the pupils gives him a drink.

The Magician now realizes what has happened. He is indignant and at the same time alarmed. Having walked agitatedly up and down the room several times, he seats himself on a chair and reflects deeply. Suddenly he gets up and gives an order to the assistant and to the pupils.

They carry out his instructions rapidly. They move a table into the centre of the room and clear the space around it. From the inner room they bring various things; certain vestments, various appurtenances, and the wand on its cushion. They cover the table with a white cloth on the border of which are embroidered astronomical signs and chemical formulas.

The Magician robes himself. He draws maniples over his hands; puts on a special girdle and a peculiar kind of covering on his feet, resembling rubber. On his head he puts a kind of crown, a broad fillet with three cones, the sharp ends pointing upwards. Over his coat he puts a robe resembling a chasuble. Meanwhile the pupils, under the direction of the Magician's assistant also get

ready, putting similar coverings on their feet, and gir-
dles round their waists. They wash their hands, shaking
them downwards a few times, and then take some kind
of drink.

The Magician is now ready. He takes a vessel like a
large bowl and places it in front of him; another vessel
of similar shape, but smaller, he puts at the opposite
end of the table. The two vessels are connected by a
copper bar. The pupils hand him a liquid which he pours
into the vessel. Around the first vessel stand nine candles, six are alight and three are unlighted. Having taken
the wand in his left hand, the Magician makes certain
movements with his right hand, and pronounces some
unknown words. At the same time four of the pupils,
two men on the right and two girls on the left, make
passes above the smaller vessel. It is noticeable how
soon they become exhausted doing this. Immediately
they are replaced by other pairs. Gradually the larger
vessel begins to emit light from within. At the moment
when this light first appears, the three unlighted candles light up. Every time the Magician brings the wand
near to the vessel a spark appears, and as time goes on
the spark grows stronger and stronger. The candles and
the symbol above the throne burn more brightly. The
ceremony continues. The movements of the Magician
become ever more energetic and intense. The noise

45

within the vessel increases, and, at the moment of greatest uproar, there is a terrible crackling within the vessel, and a fearful explosion takes place.

Immediately there is complete darkness, after which, by degrees, a half-light returns, and on the back wall a picture appears showing a portion of the cave of the Black Magician, who, seated on his throne, contorts himself making convulsive movements. The White Magician continues his manipulations. Again there is a terrific explosion, followed by an echo from behind the scenes, and accompanied by shrill whistling sounds and great uproar. The Black Magician falls in convulsions from his throne. There is again a moment of complete darkness and oppressive silence, after which the light returns and the picture of the cave disappears.

The White Magician is greatly exhausted; the pupils who assisted him are no less spent than he, but the work continues. Quickly they take away the vessels and candles from the table. They remove the table and in its place they put an armchair in which the Magician seats himself. Around him stand the pupils. The Magician, holding the wand in his hand, closes his eyes and whispers some words with concentration. Gradually the light grows dim again. Another picture appears. It shows a part of Gafar's room. He is half-lying on the divan and with an expression of joy and self-satisfaction looks towards the inner room. Apparently he expects someone.

Zeinab enters with a woman, who, bowing low before Gafar, motions with her hand towards Zeinab and immediately goes out backwards.

Gafar rises, takes Zeinab by the hand and is about to seat her on the divan, when all at once, with a sudden start they both become rooted to the spot in exactly those postures in which they were standing. After a short pause, they turn, like automata, and go out of the room.

The streets and alleys through which they pass like sleeping people, flash by. The picture vanishes. The former light again returns, and at this moment Gafar and Zeinab enter. Both are in a somnambulistic state. At their appearance the Magician, with a sigh of relief, gets up and begins to disrobe. The assistant with some of the pupils place Gafar and also Zeinab on chairs, and awaken Zeinab.

Zeinab, on coming to herself, asks those around her what is the matter. They explain what has happened, pointing to the sleeping Gafar. She suddenly remembers, bursts into sobs, and with gestures of penitence, throws herself at the feet of the Magician.

He, having finished his disrobing, bends down to her, and stroking her hair, raises her from the ground. Then he goes to Gafar who has already come to himself. Gafar is at first dumbfounded, but, learning what has happened, he grows excited and almost threatens the Magician. The latter with a calm smile answers him. Gafar listens and gradually becomes more composed. The Magician continues to talk, accompanying his words with gestures and pointing to the back of the room where once more a picture appears.

A street with a crowd of people is seen; there are women, children and old people. From a side street comes Gafar; he is old, bent and feeble. He is followed by some bright being. In spite of his age, Gafar is evidently very happy and cheerful. In the crowd he is greeted by everyone, women and men bow low to him and children bring him flowers. All is joy, happiness and blessing.

The Magician goes on speaking. The picture changes.

The same street with a crowd of people. Again Gafar appears, but this time he is accompanied by a terrible being of dark red hue. Gafar is an old man with an evil and dissatisfied face. Those who meet him turn aside with aversion and spit in his footsteps; the boys throw stones at him; their disgust is plain, and it is obvious that everyone is revolted by the sight of him.

The picture vanishes. The Magician continues to speak. Gafar is evidently perturbed and overwhelmed by some inner struggle.

48

The chief point of what the Magician has said is this: As you sow, so shall you reap. The deeds of the present determine the future; all that is good and all that is bad; both are results of the past. It is the duty of every man in every moment of the present to prepare the future, improving on the past. Such is the law of fate. And 'May the source of all laws be blessed.'

At this moment the light again becomes dim; some movement is seen. When the light returns, the assistant is standing on the Magician's right and Zeinab on his left; she is kissing the hand of the Magician. Gafar is at his feet in an attitude of reverence. Around the throne and about the room the pupils stand in various attitudes.

The Magician raises his right hand aloft. He looks upwards and whispers these words as if in prayer:

'Lord Creator, and all you His assistants, help us to be able to remember ourselves at all times in order that we may avoid involuntary actions, as only through them can evil manifest itself.'

All sing, 'Forces become transformed to be.'

The Magician again blesses them all with both hands and says. 'May reconciliation, hope, diligence and justice be ever with you all.'

All sing, 'Amen.'

Curtain.

www.ingramcontent.com/pod-product-compliance
Lightning Source LLC
Chambersburg PA
CBHW060750100426
42813CB00004B/767